What Is Predestination?

Crucial Questions booklets provide a quick introduction to definitive Christian truths. This expanding collection includes titles such as:

Who Is Jesus?

Can I Trust the Bible?

Does Prayer Change Things?

Can I Know God's Will?

How Should I Live in This World?

What Does It Mean to Be Born Again?

Can I Be Sure I'm Saved?

What Is Faith?

What Can I Do with My Guilt?

What Is the Trinity?

TO BROWSE THE REST OF THE SERIES, PLEASE VISIT: REFORMATIONTRUST.COM/CQ

CQ

What Is Predestination?

R.C. SPROUL

IR *Reformation Trust*   A DIVISION OF LIGONIER MINISTRIES, ORLANDO, FL

What Is Predestination?
© 2019 by R.C. Sproul

Published by Reformation Trust Publishing
a division of Ligonier Ministries
421 Ligonier Court, Sanford, FL 32771
Ligonier.org   ReformationTrust.com

Printed in China
RR Donnelley
0000819
First edition

ISBN 978-1-64289-143-0 (Paperback)
ISBN 978-1-64289-144-7 (ePub)
ISBN 978-1-64289-145-4 (Kindle)

Cover design: Ligonier Creative
Interior typeset: Katherine Lloyd, The DESK

Scripture quotations are from the ESV® Bible (The Holy Bible, English Standard Version®), copyright © 2001 by Crossway, a publishing ministry of Good News Publishers. Used by permission. All rights reserved.

Library of Congress Cataloging-in-Publication Data

Names: Sproul, R.C. (Robert Charles), 1939-2017, author.
Title: What is predestination? / by R.C. Sproul.
Description: Orlando : Reformation Trust, 2019. | Series: Crucial Questions ;
   No. 31
Identifiers: LCCN 2018051625| ISBN 9781642891430 (pbk.) | ISBN
   9781642891454 (kindle)
Subjects: LCSH: Predestination.
Classification: LCC BT810.3 .S67 2019 | DDC 234/.9--dc23
LC record available at https://lccn.loc.gov/2018051625

Contents

Chapter One

The Inevitable Question

No doctrine in the Christian faith engenders more debate than the doctrine of predestination. On seminary campuses and now especially online, people display a fiendish delight and inherent fascination with this doctrine, and it has fueled many midnight discussions and fierce social media debates.

Not only are people significantly divided over their views of predestination, they're also profoundly divided on how the doctrine should be treated. Some are convinced that, like religion and politics, it should never be discussed in polite company. Such people view predestination as a topic that ends in godless controversy and useless debate, and they think it has no value in terms of spiritual edification. Others believe that the doctrine of predestination is fundamentally important to a complete perspective of our relationship to God and our salvation, and they consider it wickedly neglectful to ignore or denigrate its importance in any way.

Martin Luther affirmed the central place of predestination and the importance of teaching it. He called it the *core ecclesia*, meaning "the heart of the church." While Luther was at times given to overstatements and hyperbole, this is not such an instance. No other doctrine more clearly demonstrates our utter dependence on divine grace and mercy than the doctrine of predestination. No other doctrine is more comforting to the personal struggle of faith than the doctrine of election.

All the saints of history who believed that predestination belongs at the very heart of our understanding of Christianity—Augustine, Luther, John Calvin, and Jonathan Edwards—believed just as strongly that great care must be taken in handling the doctrine, for it can be easily distorted and seriously misunderstood. Such misunderstandings can lead people into such a distorted view of God that He becomes almost demonic.

Much is at stake in how we understand predestination, and we must be extraordinarily sensitive and careful in how we handle this doctrine. It is profoundly important to our understanding of the character of God, His grace, and our own salvation, yet it is a volatile issue, and one by which many people have run into ruin by their lack of care in understanding it.

Historically, virtually every denomination and every church that has a confession of faith or creed has developed some doctrine of predestination. We cannot say that Presbyterians believe in predestination and Methodists don't, or that Episcopalians believe in predestination but Roman Catholics don't. Every church and every Christian has some doctrine of predestination because the Bible has a doctrine of predestination. Any church body or individual Christian who takes seriously the contents of the New Testament must sooner or later struggle with this doctrine.

The word *predestination* wasn't invented by Augustine or Luther or Calvin. It is found in the New Testament itself, and therefore, it is not peculiar to a movement in church history after the Apostolic age. The word refers to a biblical concept, and anyone who is convinced of the authority of Scripture must recognize that in order to submit to the Apostolic word, one must have some understanding of the doctrine of predestination.

Suppose for a moment that it is the first century AD, and you are a member of the Christian community. You long for a word from Christ, an authoritative teaching, and you know that the chief Apostle to the gentiles is Saul of Tarsus. Word has just arrived that a circuit rider has appeared in Ephesus with a letter from the hand of the Apostle Paul addressed to all the Christians. A special gathering is held for the epistle to be read aloud, and you are hearing it for the first time.

You've never had an argument about predestination. You've never been involved in a theological discussion. You're simply a new Christian in Ephesus, and you hear the following greeting: "Paul, an apostle of Christ Jesus by the will of God, to the saints who are in Ephesus, and are faithful in Christ Jesus: Grace to you and peace from God our Father and the Lord Jesus Christ" (Eph. 1:1–2). Then the body of the letter begins: "Blessed be the God and Father of our Lord Jesus Christ, who has blessed us in

Christ with every spiritual blessing in the heavenly places, even as he chose us in him before the foundation of the world" (vv. 3–4).

The very first statement of the body of the epistle announces that you have been chosen by God before the very foundation of the world. Does that get your attention? Paul did not tack on this statement as a postscript at the end of his epistle. Instead, he jumps to it right at the beginning. The letter continues: "Even as he chose us in him before the foundation of the world, that we should be holy and blameless before him. In love he predestined us for adoption to himself as sons through Jesus Christ, according to the purpose of his will, to the praise of his glorious grace, with which he has blessed us in the Beloved" (vv. 4–6). In verse 11, Paul says, "In him we have obtained an inheritance, having been predestined according to the purpose of him who works all things according to the counsel of his will."

At the very outset of this epistle, Paul plunges into the depths and the riches of the doctrine of predestination. In fact, he makes it central to his teaching. Predestination does not refer to the course of the stars, God's general divine superintendence, His providence over the universe, or His governance over natural laws. Rather, Paul is talking about salvation—a predestined salvation in which, from the foundation of the world, believers were chosen by God to be saved.

What are we to make of this? If we are to grow in maturity in Christ, we must understand the biblical teaching on predestination. We may not like it at first, but with careful study and attention to the witness of Scripture, we can come to see the doctrine's sweetness and its excellence and to experience it as a great comfort to our souls.

Chapter Two

What Is Predestination?

We must start by asking a seemingly simple question: What is predestination? There appear to be as many different definitions of predestination as there are doctrines of predestination. Since the Bible was not written in English, we don't find the English word *predestination*, yet multiple Greek words convey the concept, so we look to these Greek words to inform our understanding of what predestination means.

One example is the Greek word *proorizō*. The prefix *pro-* corresponds to the English prefix *pre-*, meaning something that takes place in advance, in front of, or before something else that follows later, while *orizō* means "to appoint, designate, assign." Therefore, *proorizō* refers to ordaining or designating something beforehand.

Without being fatalists, thinking that everything that happens falls out according to some impersonal guiding principle, we can say that we each have a destiny. In God's providence, that destiny is in His hand and in His eternal plan. Before any of us were born, our destinies were written by God before the foundation of the earth.

With respect to salvation, the doctrine of predestination does not include the concept that every detail of our lives is foreordained and predestined by God. Rather, this doctrine deals with our ultimate destiny. Certainly, every detail of our lives is foreordained by God, but that truth belongs more properly to the doctrine of God's providence. The doctrine of predestination, in its initial form, does not include these particular elements in its scope (though they are true). It simply concerns our final destiny and where we will go when we die.

Most Christians will agree that God is not simply a

spectator of human events, but that He does, at least in some ways, decide things in advance. Most would affirm that in at least some sense, God has what we call *foreknowledge,* as this concept is deeply rooted in the pages of Scripture. God knows all things in advance, and He knows them perfectly. But as soon as we begin to probe the extent of that foreknowledge and the grounds for that foreknowledge, Christians divide into opposite camps and the philosophical debates erupt.

Though all churches and Christians don't agree about the nature of predestination, one point can be agreed on: God, in His sovereignty, in some way predestines who gets to heaven and who does not. That's the simplest definition of predestination. The focal point of predestination is the doctrine of election we find in the New Testament, and that has to do with God's choosing and making a decision about heaven or hell.

Virtually all Christians believe that much about predestination. But exactly how God makes the decision in advance about our ultimate destiny is by no means a matter of universal agreement among professing Christians or in the historic creeds. There are many different doctrines of predestination. While delving into all the subtle nuances and peculiarities of the various views is beyond the scope of this book, we must mention the two most common views of predestination that we find in church history.

The first of these most common views—and perhaps the majority view in the Christian world today—is the prescient view. *Prescience* is simply a synonym for *foreknowledge*. The prescient view of predestination holds that God, from all eternity, looks down the corridors of history and knows in advance who will and will not respond positively to the invitation of Christ and His gospel. He knows that some will say yes to Christ and others will say no. From all eternity, God ordains that every person who says yes to the gospel will go to heaven. He chooses them for heaven based on their foreseen faith.

The Augustinian view, also called the Reformation view, holds that God, from all eternity, not only predestines those who will believe to be *saved*, but He also predestines those who will believe to *believe*. In other words, apart from God's predestinating grace, no one would ever believe. People are not predestined to heaven because they believe or because God knows that they will believe; they are predestined to believe that they might go to heaven.

The Augustinian view maintains that from the foundation of the world—before anyone was born or did anything—God decided who would be brought to faith and who would not. Eternal destiny is rooted and grounded in God's predestinating grace. Those who are not predestined from the foundation of the world will not come to faith, and their destination will not be heaven.

These two views are very different. In the first view, the decisive factor regarding a person's destiny rests with the individual. In the second view, the decisive factor rests with God. Those who take the latter view must respond to questions about God's fairness and justice and about man's free will. Those who take the first view must answer the question of why is it that some people say yes and others say no. Is it because some people are more righteous, intelligent, or meritorious than others?

Studying predestination forces us to ask and answer hard questions, and if nothing else, it forces us to look more closely at the character of God and at our own sinfulness. We can never spend too much time studying the character of God. There is no such thing as a "too developed" understanding of the grace of God or the greatness of God. Nor is it harmful to us to explore the depths of our own human weakness. Virtually all of the errors that plague the church and her doctrine relate to one of two errors: either an underestimation of the greatness of God or an overestimation of the greatness of man.

Chapter Three

The Golden Chain

The biblical text that is perhaps used most often to support the doctrine of prescience—the idea that election is based on God's foreknowledge—is found in Paul's letter to the Romans. Chapter 8 contains the classic statements used to support the concept of prescience: "For those whom he foreknew he also predestined to be conformed to the image of his Son, in order that he might be the firstborn among many brothers. And those whom he predestined he also called, and those whom he called he also justified, and those whom he justified he also glorified" (vv. 29–30).

These verses are often called the "golden chain of salvation" because they contain a series of redemptive actions or events, a shorthand version of what theologians call the *ordo salutis* or the order of salvation. The order of salvation has something in common with the question of the chicken and the egg: What comes (at least logically) first?

According to Romans 8:29, this order starts with foreknowledge: "those whom he foreknew." Advocates of the prescient view of predestination consider this an extremely significant point, arguing that God's election is based on His foreknowledge of future events and the choices that human beings will make.

However, the text does not explicitly say that those whom He foreknew He predestined *on the basis of His foreknowledge*. All it says is that those whom He foreknew He also predestined. The prescient view assumes that predestination is based in some way on foreknowledge. However, this is an inference from the text and not necessarily justified.

In terms of temporal priority, we are on more solid ground. The Apostle Paul often mentions things in lists.

For example, he gives a series of ideas like the fruit of the Spirit or the gifts of the Spirit. We should not look at these scriptural lists and impose a certain priority on them unless the text explicitly gives priority of importance to the various ideas. We also should not assume that the items occur in a certain temporal sequence just because they appear in a list.

In this case with Romans 8, it safe to assume that there is a priority in the list, particularly if we go to the end of the list of events described here and work backward. The last item mentioned is "glorification." In terms of working out our salvation, we know from other passages of Scripture that the sequential steps are faith, justification, sanctification, and glorification. This order cannot be rearranged. Therefore, it is safe to assume here (though Paul does not mention sanctification in the list in Romans 8) that the text contains a sequential ordering, since it begins with foreknowledge in eternity past and ends with glorification in the future.

Additional assumptions can be made in regard to this text. Notice that the text does not explicitly state the following: "*All* of those who are foreknown are predestined, and *all* of those who are predestined are called, and *all* of those who are called are justified, and *all* of those who are justified are glorified." However, the text appears to be elliptical, meaning it is assuming something without stating it explicitly, namely, the word *all*.

Certainly, there are solid biblical grounds to believe that all who are justified are glorified. This *all* is a necessary implication of the text. However, if this is true, it raises serious problems for the prescient view.

Let's suppose for a moment that the word *all* is not proper to insert in this passage, and instead, the word *some* is put in its place: "*Some* who are foreknown are predestined. *Some* who are predestined are called. *Some* who are called are justified. *Some* who are justified are glorified." In this scenario, the problems are glaring with respect to everything the Bible teaches about the final destination of justified and predestined people. Some who are predestined would not be justified; some of the elect would not be glorified. Inserting the word *some* destroys both the classical Augustinian view of predestination unto salvation as well as the prescient view of predestination.

It is much better to understand this passage as denoting universal categories in this golden chain: *all* who are foreknown (in whatever sense one understands foreknowledge here) are predestined, and *all* who are predestined are called, and *all* who are called are justified, and *all* who are justified are glorified.

What did the Apostle Paul have in mind when he talked about those who are "called"? The Bible, after all, uses the word *call* in more than one way. For example, Jesus said, "For many are called, but few are chosen" (Matt. 22:14). To answer this question, we must distinguish between the *external* call of God and the *internal* call of God.

The external call is the basic proclamation of the gospel message to all people. Some respond positively; others reject it. When Paul spoke on Mars Hill to the Athenian philosophers (Acts 17:16–34), some mocked him and rejected his teaching, while others gladly received his announcement of the resurrection. A third category of people wanted to mull it over and give more consideration to Paul's words. Paul outwardly called everyone present to repent and receive Christ, but not all responded to this outward call. In fact, the gospel is preached to many people who do not obey the summons of God or respond positively to the call of God to Christ.

The internal call, however, has to do with the secret operation of the Holy Spirit. He calls men and women inwardly, changes the dispositions of their hearts, raises them to new spiritual life, awakens them from their dog-matic slumbers, and impels them toward faith and belief. That's what is meant by the inward call of God.

The question is, Which of these is in view in this text when Paul says that those whom God calls He justifies? If the call referred to in this passage is the external call, that would mean everyone who hears the external call is justi-fied, and that everyone who hears the gospel has faith. But we know this is not the case. Therefore, this passage cannot refer to the external call; it can refer only to the internal call. Only those who respond inwardly to the outward call of the gospel are justified. We can, therefore, safely con-clude that when the text says, "those whom he called he also justified," it is referring to the internal call.

Notice that in this sequence, the internal call comes after foreknowledge and after predestination. The pre-scient view argues that God knows in advance all who will respond to the outward call of the gospel, and on the basis of this knowledge, He predestinates them to justification and glorification. In order to accommodate this view, the order in the chain would have to be rearranged.

The Augustinian position, however, is that God pre-destines people to an inward call by the Holy Spirit, and everyone whom God predestines unto salvation will be called, justified, and glorified. The Augustinian view holds that God cannot predestine anyone, for any reason, to anything of which He has no knowledge. God does not predestine unknown people. Obviously, foreknowledge must be first in any succession of the decrees of God, since He doesn't decree anything for anyone of whom He knows nothing.

The natural sequence of the golden chain is that predestination follows foreknowledge—not in the sense that it's based on God's knowing what people will choose when left to themselves, but that foreknowledge must precede anything that God decrees with respect to individuals. The Bible doesn't say that predestination is based on God's prior knowledge of what people will do. It is based on God's prior knowledge of people. The elect are predestined to be called—and *all* who are predestined to be called are called, and *all* who are called are justified, and *all* who are justified are glorified. No one in the group of the elect will fail to be elect. All the text is saying is that God's predestination includes a knowledge in advance of the objects of His predestinating work—the people.

If we look carefully at the golden chain, which is appealed to over and over by those who want to base predestination on foreknowledge in the sense of foreknown human responses, the chain actually turns that argument on its ear. Romans 8:29–30 is one of the most powerful passages in all of Scripture in favor of the Augustinian view.

To summarize, the Apostle Paul teaches in Romans 8 that all of the elect are foreknown by God. There is no election apart from foreknowledge. Predestination means that people are predestined to be called, justified, and glorified. Interestingly, this golden chain comes immediately after a marvelous verse from which many believers draw comfort: "And we know that for those who love God all things work together for good, for those who are called according to his purpose" (Rom. 8:28). That is, all things are working together through the divine hand of providence for the elect, because it is God's eternal plan to ensure the complete redemption of those whom He has predestined to salvation.

Chapter Four

The Divine Choice

What factor ultimately determines a person's salvation? Is it the human decision and response, which God knows in advance, or is it God's sovereign election, in which He brings people to faith in Jesus Christ? That is the essence of the controversy over predestination.

Someone once noted, "All people are by nature Pelagian." By this, he meant that people naturally believe that man is not fundamentally enslaved by sin as a result of the fall of Adam, and that they still have the power in their fallen natures (if they believe they're fallen at all) to incline themselves toward faith and make a decision for Christ.

Almost all contemporary evangelism presupposes the moral ability of sinners to incline their own hearts to a positive response to the gospel. Regeneration does not automatically eliminate that kind of thinking from our minds. Many Christians assume that when they became Christians, they were the ones who did it. They know that they could not be redeemed apart from the grace of God or the work of Jesus Christ, but they assume that the reason they believed, while their friends persisted in unbelief, was that they made the right decision and their friends made the wrong decision. Such Christians assume that somehow they, not God, were the decisive factor.

However, personal experience is not ultimate or determinative—Scripture is. So, we must closely examine the Apostle Paul's words on the subject in Romans 9.

Paul begins the chapter by swearing an oath—a somber thing for an Apostle to do. His readers would have understood that he was laying his integrity on the line in making an oath concerning his feelings about those who are not being saved. Particularly, he's concerned about the first-century Israelites who had rejected Christ. Shockingly, he swears an oath that he would be willing to lose his own salvation if it meant the salvation of his kinsmen according to the flesh.

After lamenting the failure of his kinsmen to come to faith, Paul writes:

> For I could wish that I myself were accursed and cut off from Christ for the sake of my brothers, my kinsmen according to the flesh. They are Israelites, and to them belong the adoption, the glory, the covenants, the giving of the law, the worship, and the promises. To them belong the patriarchs, and from their race, according to the flesh, is the Christ, who is God over all, blessed forever. Amen.
>
> But it is not as though the word of God has failed. For not all who are descended from Israel belong to Israel, and not all are children of Abraham because they are his offspring, but "Through Isaac shall your offspring be named." This means that it is not the children of the flesh who are the children of God, but the children of the promise are counted as offspring. For this is what the promise said: "About this time next year I will return, and Sarah shall have a son." (Rom. 9:3–9)

Paul is reminding his listeners about the history of Israel. Not everyone who was a physical child of Abraham was chosen by God to receive the blessing. Ishmael was born of Abraham, but he did not receive the blessing—Isaac did. We can go back further and look at Abraham himself. Why did God come to Abraham while he was a pagan, living in a pagan country, practicing a pagan religion (Josh. 24:2–3)? God unilaterally revealed Himself to Abraham, moved him out of that environment, and used him to create a whole new seed of redemption.

Why did Christ appear to Saul of Tarsus, the avowed enemy of the church, who was breathing out fire on a mission to wipe out the Christian community? Why did Christ appear to him on the road to Damascus in glory and change him instantly? Why didn't He do that for Pontius Pilate, Caiaphas, or Annas? It's clear from the history of redemption that Abraham received a measure of grace that other people in the Old Testament did not, and that likewise, Paul received a measure of grace that other people in the New Testament did not.

Paul reaches the most salient point in Romans 9:10–11: "And not only so, but also when Rebekah had conceived children by one man, our forefather Isaac, though they were not yet born and had done nothing either good or bad—in order that God's purpose of election might continue." Paul is clearly saying here that something happened before the children were born, before they had done any good or evil. And then he states the purpose: "in order that God's purpose of election might continue."

The passage goes on to say, "She was told, 'The older will serve the younger.' As it is written, 'Jacob I loved, but Esau I hated'" (vv. 12–13). Then we read, "So then it depends not on human will or exertion, but on God, who has mercy. For the Scripture says to Pharaoh, 'For this very purpose I have raised you up, that I might show my power in you, and that my name might be proclaimed in all the earth.' So then he has mercy on whomever he wills, and he hardens whomever he wills" (vv. 16–18).

The prescient view argues that God looked down the corridors of time before Esau and Jacob were born, and on the basis of knowing how they would behave, He chose Jacob and not Esau. Yet that argument flies in the face of the clear teaching of the Apostle.

In Romans 9, Paul labors the point that our election is not based on what we do— not on our doing, our willing, our goodness, or our badness. Instead, before we were born—and without any respect to what we would do or not do—God elected some and not others, that His purposes in election might stand. It's fascinating to note that God didn't just distinguish between two different people, cultures, lands, and religions; He distinguished between sons of the same father in the same family. Further, they were not just brothers but twins. Paul uses this illustration to drive home the point that this was done to show the purpose of God's electing mercy and to make absolutely clear that our election is based "not on human will or exertion" but on the sovereignty of God.

Some try to get around this text by saying that Paul is not speaking here about the election of individuals. Instead, they say, he is talking about the election of nations—that out of Jacob came the nation of Israel and out of Esau came the Edomites. However, this argument is easily refuted. Nations are simply groups made up of individuals, and in the passage, Paul specifically speaks with respect to individuals. One individual was chosen, and another was not. Neither was chosen or not chosen because of anything he did or would ever do. The Apostle Paul labors to show that Jacob's election was based on the sovereign purposes of God in order to display His grace.

Note Paul's immediate response to what he has been teaching. He anticipates the question that is raised every time this doctrine is taught: "How is it fair if God chooses one and not the other, if it's not based on what we do? If it were based on what we do, at least that would be fair." Paul responds to this hypothetical question by saying, "What shall we say then? Is there injustice on God's part? By no means!" (v. 14). Other translations read, "God forbid!" The Greek phrase used here is the most emphatic term of denial possible. The answer that Paul gives to the question, "Is there injustice on God's part?" is, "Absolutely not!"

Paul's anticipation of such an objection would not have been necessary if the text were teaching the prescient view. If God's election were based on what we do, no one would raise a voice of protest or accuse God of being unfair. Our view of fairness stems from our belief that people should be judged according to their behavior, so Paul knew that people would struggle with the teaching that in the case of Jacob and Esau, their respective destinies were planned from the foundation of the world by God according to His sovereign counsel, without any respect to anything either one of them ever did or would do.

When unbelievers hear the teaching found in Romans

9, they often say something like this: "Well, I'm not a believer, so why should I even be concerned? If I'm not elect, and if I'm not going to be saved, why should I bother?" The response to that is this: to any who do not at this moment have faith in Jesus Christ, there is no reason whatsoever to assume you are not elect. Every person who has ever come to faith in Christ was at one time an unbeliever. You may very well be numbered among the elect but have not yet realized your election.

One of the most important admonitions in the New Testament is that we make our election and calling sure (2 Peter 1:10). For all who are uncertain whether they're numbered among the elect, there is no more important question to focus your attention on until an answer is found.

Chapter Five

Justice, Mercy, and Grace

The doctrines surrounding the Augustinian view of election are also referred to as the "doctrines of grace." This designation rightly puts the accent where it belongs, since the focal point of the biblical doctrine of election is the grace of God. But what exactly is grace?

In its simplest terms, grace can be defined as "unmerited favor." When we receive grace from God, we receive a blessing, favor, or benefit from His hand that we have not deserved, earned, or merited. It comes to us simply from the wideness of His mercy. The Apostle Paul appeals to the mercy of God when the question, "Is there injustice on God's part?" is raised (Rom. 9:14). He reminds his readers—Christians living in Rome—what God had already revealed to Moses in the Old Testament: "I will have mercy on whom I have mercy, and I will have compassion on whom I have compassion" (v. 15). So, the first thing we must understand about God's grace is that His grace is sovereign. Grace is something that God is never obligated to give—God doesn't owe anyone grace.

If God owed us grace, it would no longer be grace. It would simply be justice. Justice is receiving one's due as a reward or a punishment for certain forms of behavior. Grace, however, is not required. God reserves the right of cosmic executive clemency. It is executive privilege on His part. He can be merciful to whom He wants to be merciful, and He can withhold His mercy or His grace from whomever He decides to withhold it from, for whatever reason He is inclined to do so, in order to accomplish His purposes.

When Paul asks, "Is there injustice on God's part?" the answer is, "By no means!" (v. 14). Yet what if we ask the question somewhat differently: Is there *nonjustice* on God's part? The answer to that question is yes. There is nonjustice in God, though there is not *injustice* in Him.

There are different kinds of nonjustice—two of which are most important for our consideration. On the one hand, there is *injustice*. On the other hand, there is *mercy* or *grace*. *Injustice* is a category of evil that is absolutely antithetical to justice. If God ever did anything that was unjust, He would no longer be a righteous God. He would no longer be good. But consider *mercy* or *grace*. Is there anything wrong with a holy, righteous God being gracious or merciful? It would not be evil for a just and righteous Being to grant mercy or grace, because grace and mercy are laudable.

Suppose we have a group of seven people. When we talk about the doctrine of election, we understand that some people receive the grace of election and some do not. Imagine that four of these people receive grace, and the other three receive justice from God's hand. That is, the elect receive the grace of God, and the nonelect receive the justice of God. Have any of these people been a victim of God's injustice? Of course not. That is what Paul is getting at when he asks the question, "Is there injustice on God's part?"

The question is asked because God's grace is not given equally to everyone. Because God gives a gracious gift to Jacob that He doesn't give to Esau, this seems unfair. The protest goes like this: If God gives grace to one person, then He must give grace to everyone else. That just seems fair.

However, let's consider a hypothetical case of two prisoners who have been convicted of first-degree murder. The governor decides to exercise executive clemency and pardon one of those criminals. That criminal does not deserve to be pardoned. He deserves to be executed, but he escapes justice, and he receives mercy. Suppose also that the governor does not choose to pardon the other convicted murderer; instead, the second murderer is punished. Has he been unjustly punished? Of course not. He receives justice.

Is it necessary that if the governor pardons one that he must therefore pardon all? What law states that if one receives mercy, then all must receive mercy? That would be necessary only if justice required it, but we are not talking about justice. We are talking about nonjustice. We're talking about mercy and grace. This is what Paul emphatically reminds the readers of Romans—that God had already said to Moses, "I will have mercy on whom I have mercy, and I will have compassion on whom I have compassion."

This is one of the most crucial concepts to under-stand about biblical Christianity, yet it's one that few ever grasp. Most Christians believe that God is sovereign. Yet when you begin to probe and ask people how they under-stand the sovereignty of God, it's not long before there's not very much sovereignty left in God. When people say they believe in God's sovereignty, they often mean that they believe God has authority and power over His cre-ation (and that is indeed an aspect of God's sovereignty). But when the topic of the sovereignty of grace comes up, people don't want to believe that God has the authority or the right to grant His mercy and grace as He wills. That is what's at stake in this discussion.

If God were committing injustice in all of this, the pro-test would be understandable. If God looked at a world filled with innocent people and decided to save some and damn others, there would be injustice on God's part, but only once in all of history has God punished an innocent man. But even here we need a qualification. That punish-ment occurred only after the innocent man willingly, for the sake of the elect, assumed the culpability of the sin of His people. When our sins were transferred to Jesus, before the bar of God's justice, Jesus was no longer innocent. He was innocent in and of Himself, but by imputation, as our representative, He was regarded as sin (see 2 Cor. 5:21).

In one sense, the greatest concentration of wickedness that ever occurred on this planet was on the cross, where Christ took the sins and guilt of an untold multitude on Himself. It was only after that transfer, to which He was willing to submit, that He bore the just wrath of God. In reality, God has never, ever punished an innocent person, because it would be unrighteous and unjust for Him to do that.

When we think about this difficult question of election and God's choosing, we must understand that when God makes His decision, when He is contemplating those whom He will save or not save, He is contemplating them as fallen people. God's question is not, "Am I going to rescue some innocent people and allow other innocent people to perish?" Rather, His question, like the governor's question, is, "Am I going to exercise grace and mercy to some guilty people and allow others to receive My justice?" The beauty in this is that in God's sovereign election, His marvelous grace and mercy are manifested, and His relentless commitment to justice is also revealed.

It is easy enough to define grace as "unmerited favor," but to get this idea from our brains into our bloodstream is one of the most difficult tasks in the Christian life. To get it to stay there is even more difficult. The moment we begin to think that God owes us, or anyone, mercy is the moment we should have a bell go off in our brains. We need a warning that we are no longer thinking about mercy, because again, mercy that is required is not mercy. If we think that God owes us grace, we've stopped thinking about grace and have started thinking about justice. The worst thing that could happen to us is for us to ask God for justice. The only way we can draw a breath in this world, and the only way we can hope of going to heaven, is by His sovereign grace alone.

Chapter Six

For His Good Pleasure

We have been wrestling with some significant questions in our study of predestination. Why does God elect certain people and not others? Why is it that some receive His grace while others receive His justice? So far, we've seen that no one receives injustice at the hand of God; His mercy and grace are always His sovereign privilege to bestow as He sees fit and for whatever reason He's inclined to do so.

In this chapter, we return to the book of Ephesians to

explore the idea of God's giving grace to some and not to others. Paul has already made clear that election is not based on people's own actions, but instead, it is based purely on the purposes of God. In Ephesians 1:3–12, we read:

Blessed be the God and Father of our Lord Jesus Christ, who has blessed us in Christ with every spiritual blessing in the heavenly places, even as he chose us in him before the foundation of the world, that we should be holy and blameless before him. In love he predestined us for adoption to himself as sons through Jesus Christ, according to the purpose of his will, to the praise of his glorious grace, with which he has blessed us in the Beloved. In him we have redemption through his blood, the forgiveness of our trespasses, according to the riches of his grace, which he lavished upon us, in all wisdom and insight making known to us the mystery of his will, according to his purpose, which he set forth in Christ as a plan for the fullness of time, to unite all things in him, things in heaven and things on earth. In him we have obtained an inheritance, having been predestined according to the purpose of him who works all things according to the counsel of his will, so that we who were the first to hope in Christ might be to the praise of his glory.

In light of this text, it is astonishing that so many controversies over the sovereignty of grace have continued in the church throughout the centuries. Paul could not spell it out with any greater clarity than he does here in Ephesians. Clearly, God sovereignly elects some to salvation and does not elect others; He chooses some people as objects of His saving grace and tremendous benefits but does not give that same blessing and favor to others. That being the case, the question is, Is God's choice arbitrary or capricious? He may not be unjust, but He certainly appears arbitrary in this regard.

To address that question, we must first define our terms. What do *arbitrary* and *capricious* mean? An arbitrary or capricious person acts without any particular reason for doing so. When asked why he did a particular thing, such a person would respond: "No reason. I just did it on a whim." We don't tend to respect people who do things for no reason. Are we going to attribute to God that kind of unvirtuous behavior?

Based on what we have said thus far, some might argue that we *must* attribute these characteristics to God. After all, we have labored the point that God chooses people for no reason in them, foreseen or otherwise. That is true. God's reason for choosing some for salvation has nothing to do with anything in any particular person. His grace is given not for any reason in us.

The fact that there is no reason in *us* does not mean there is no reason *at all* behind God's actions. When the Bible makes clear that the reason for our election is not in us, it does not mean that God is being capricious or arbitrary. Instead, the Bible repeats over and over that God has reasons for doing so, and a few words in particular recur when Scripture explains God's purpose.

One of these words is God's *counsel*—the counsel of His will. This has to do with the wisdom, plan, or thought processes of God. The very word *counsel* suggests an intelligent reason for acting. God never wills apart from His own counsel. A person who is completely arbitrary has no counsel, takes no counsel, and listens to no counsel. He simply acts on impulse. The very word *counsel* should alert us that the biblical idea of God's sovereign grace is rooted in the wisdom of God, which is perfect. It is not irrational; it is eminently rational and far from arbitrary.

Another word used again and again in the Bible with respect to predestination and election is the word *purpose*. In the Greek, this is the word *telos*. Those familiar with the study of philosophy know that it includes several different subdivisions of thought, including metaphysics, cosmology, epistemology, ethics, and teleology. *Teleology* comes from the Greek word *telos*, which means "end, purpose, goal."

A person who does something completely arbitrarily does it for no purpose. Yet the New Testament makes clear that God has a divine purpose in electing grace. He desires to manifest the riches of His grace, to display His mercy, and to reveal something about His marvelous, awesome, and beautiful character. Another of God's purposes in election is to honor Christ, of whom the prophecy was made, "Out of the anguish of his soul he shall see and be satisfied" (Isa. 53:11).

The prescient view of election leads to the belief that Jesus died on the cross, but not for anyone in particular. Instead, He dies to make salvation a possibility for those who choose to believe. In that view, it is theoretically possible that Christ could have died completely in vain, that no one would ever have responded positively to the gospel, and that Christ would have died and not actually saved anyone. But according to Scripture, God determined from the foundation of the world that the cross of Jesus Christ would yield its appointed fruit and that Christ would see the travail of His pain, suffering, and death and be satisfied.

When the New Testament speaks of election and predestination, it always speaks of our being chosen in the Beloved, in Christ. When we look into our own hearts and lives, we cannot give any compelling answers as to why God would save people like us. We should be properly amazed by the grace of God, but tragically, we tend to take His grace for granted. Once we assume it, we begin to presume on it. Yet had God determined to treat us according to His justice, none of us would be able to stand. The only way we can gain entrance into the kingdom is through the sovereign grace of God and by that grace alone—*sola gratia.*

The only reason given in the New Testament for anyone being saved is so that God the Father can bestow His glory, love, and affection on God the Son. The only reason we're redeemed is not because of our value but because of the value of Christ. God is gracious to us in order to reward

One who does deserve a reward—His only begotten Son. This involves a strange intersection of grace and justice. It is just that Christ should receive an inheritance, and we are that inheritance. That we are the inheritance is grace for us and justice for Christ.

Why does God choose us? The New Testament answers, "in order that God's purpose of election might continue" (Rom. 9:11). It is God's purpose that we understand the graciousness of grace, that we allow it to stand, and that we are bold to proclaim it in the life of the church among God's people.

In Ephesians 1:5, we read that God "predestined us for adoption to himself as sons through Jesus Christ, *according to* the purpose of his will" (emphasis added). "According to" provides the basis, and that basis is not according to our foreseen work, merit, or righteousness. The basis of election is "the purpose of his will." One answer the Bible gives to the "why" question of election is the pleasure of God. God chooses to be gracious to some people because He takes pleasure in being gracious to some rather than to all. Does this make God capricious and arbitrary? Is He playing a cruel game of choosing some and rejecting others, of saving some and damning others?

At this point, we can easily begin to speak rashly without knowledge and come perilously close to blaspheming the Holy Spirit, because we've missed one crucial aspect of the text. The word translated "purpose" in the ESV can also be translated "good pleasure" (KJV, NKJV) or "kind intention" (NASB). What God chooses, He does so according to His *good* pleasure. This word makes all the difference in the world. There is no such thing as the bad pleasure of God's will. God does not take pleasure in evil. Human beings take pleasure in evil. In fact, that's why we sin, because it's pleasurable to us. If it weren't pleasurable, we wouldn't be enticed or tempted by it. But there is no evil will in God.

The only thing that has ever pleased God is goodness, the only pleasure that He's ever had is a good pleasure, and the only purpose that He's ever had is a good purpose. Let us never suggest that in the mystery of His grace He is capricious or arbitrary. That the reason for our salvation does not rest in us does not mean it's unreasonable and irrational or that God is without a purpose, counsel, or goodness.

It should not be hard for us to imagine that what is pleasing to God is always good, that His purposes are always good, and that His reasons for granting mercy to some and not to others have to be good. What is hard is to conceive of an evil pleasure in God or an arbitrary action of God—to imagine our sovereign Creator doing anything without a purpose or without taking into account His own omniscience, infinite knowledge, and perfect understanding of all things.

In the end, the issue is not really that we think God is arbitrary, that He acts without a purpose or does anything unjust or unrighteous. Our problem is usually that we don't always like God's decisions. We don't always agree with His counsel. We are often tempted to say or think, "If I were God, I would do this," or, "If I were God, I certainly wouldn't do that." It is at this point we must stop and repent of our arrogance. As bad as the world may sometimes seem to our finite human minds, we can say with absolute certainty that the world would be a true disaster if we were in the place of God.

Chapter Seven

The Certainty of Salvation

In the early seventeenth century, controversy erupted in the Netherlands over the doctrine of predestination. The dispute was brought on by a group called the Remonstrants, who were thus named because they remonstrated, or protested, against the Reformed doctrine of predestination. The controversy, which was addressed at the Synod of Dort in 1618–19, codified what is known as the five points of Calvinism. The answers to the five points of contention among the theologians of the day were summarized later by the famous acrostic TULIP.

This controversy centered on the difference between the classic Augustinian view of predestination unto salvation and the prescient view of predestination unto salvation. As previously noted, the prescient view holds that God looks down through the corridors of time and knows in advance who will positively respond to the gospel and embrace Christ. On the basis of that advance knowledge, God chooses those whom He knows will respond to the gospel for salvation. In other words, God elects only those who meet the condition for salvation, namely, faith.

This view of election, also called "conditional" election, is distinguished from the historic Augustinian view, which is "unconditional." In the Augustinian view, God, without foreseeing any particular conditions met by man, sovereignly and eternally chooses people unto salvation. This does not mean that salvation has no conditions—it does. Faith is required for justification. But unconditional election means that God unconditionally *chooses* the elect for salvation and sovereignly enables them to exercise the faith that meets the necessary condition for salvation.

Prominent evangelists, working out of the prescient or

conditional view of election, often employ two common metaphors in an effort to steer a careful course between two potentially dangerous concepts. On one hand, they don't want to teach that man saves himself. On the other hand, they don't want to say that salvation is totally of God. In an effort to avoid these two poles, two images are offered to help people understand the nature of salvation.

The first metaphor is that of a drowning person. He can't swim, and he is going under. Even his head is submerged below the waves, and the only thing left above the surface of the water is his hand. He cannot possibly save himself from drowning unless someone throws him a life preserver. Someone on shore then throws that life preserver exactly where the man needs to have it thrown, right up against his hand. The person on the shore has done everything that he can do to save the drowning man, but the drowning man must either grab hold of the life preserver or let it pass by. He must take his fingers and grip it, or he will drown and sink. In this scenario, God has done all He can to allow man to be saved, and man still has the power and moral strength left in himself to either grab hold of or not grab hold of salvation.

The other metaphor frequently used is that of a dying person with an incurable, fatal disease. The person is in his last stages of life. A doctor comes into the room with the only possible medicine to save this man from dying. The doctor pours the medicine on the spoon and reaches the spoon to the dying man's lips. All he must do is open his lips and receive the medicine that will restore him to fullness of health. He has the power to either keep his lips clenched tight or to open his mouth and receive the medicine. The idea is that God does 99 percent with His grace—and without that grace there's no hope of salvation. Yet there is 1 percent left to the man's ability, and that 1 percent is the decisive factor regarding His eternal destiny.

The picture of salvation in these two metaphors differs dramatically from the classic Augustinian view. One of the reasons Augustine taught that election is unconditional is that before his treatment of election, he spent a great deal of time studying the biblical view of the fall of man. He considered the question, To what degree have we been corrupted in our human nature? Augustine concluded that the fall of mankind is so great that even though we still are able to make choices, all of our choices proceed from a heart that is in bondage to sin, leaving us in a state of moral inability to choose what pleases God.

The idea that Augustine taught was this: the sinner has no

inclination in his heart for the things of God unless God first changes his soul. God must change the disposition of man's heart through the supernatural work of regeneration. Scripture says that all whom the Holy Spirit regenerates come to faith, and that this regeneration effects what it was designed to effect. Further, left to himself, man will never incline himself to the things of God, and so, if the sinner is destitute of regeneration, he will never willingly embrace Christ.

The whole point of God's work of regeneration is that God not only designs the ends of salvation, but He also ordains the means to bring about those ends in people's lives. God sovereignly determines to quicken to spiritual life those whom He has chosen, and all who are so quickened come to faith. God Himself supplies the condition necessary for the sinner to respond.

One problem with the prescient or conditional view is that it gives us something to boast about. Some people respond positively to the gospel while others do not. What is it that makes us respond positively? What allows us to fulfill the 1 percent after God has done the other 99 percent? Most people would not want to say that they are more intelligent or more righteous than their friends who have not responded. Even saying that we understand our need better is something to boast about; it means we are more spiritually sensitive or humble. The Bible says that we have nothing to boast about before God (Eph. 2:9).

The New Testament teaches that the work of salvation is utterly gracious, and it is accomplished by the sovereign grace of God. One of the most controversial texts on this topic appears in John 6:44. Jesus says: "No one can come to me unless the Father who sent me draws him. And I will raise him up on the last day." The phrase "no one" is a universal negative proposition. It says something negative about all people: "no one" means "no person whatsoever." The next word is the most crucial: "can." Jesus doesn't say that no one *does* come or no one *will* come. He says that no one *can* come.

The word "can" refers not to permission but to ability. "May" is used to describe permission, but "can" has to do with ability. In this text, Jesus says there is something that no one has the power or ability to do. And what is it? "No one can come to me." When the prescient view is deeply and carefully analyzed, it evidences an abbreviated and truncated view of the fall. It still looks at fallen man as having an "island of righteousness" left in his soul, and this island of righteousness possesses the ability to come to Christ without being regenerated by the Holy Spirit. The evangelist will say: "Come forward. Receive Christ. Choose Christ. Make a decision for Christ, and you will be born again." However, Jesus says that unless we are first born again, we will never come to Him. Rebirth is the prerequisite and the necessary condition for being able to come to Christ.

This biblical teaching is also seen in the letter to the Ephesians. The Apostle Paul writes:

> And you were dead in the trespasses and sins in which you once walked, following the course of this world, following the prince of the power of the air, the spirit that is now at work in the sons of disobedience— among whom we all once lived in the passions of our flesh, carrying out the desires of the body and the mind, and were by nature children of wrath, like the rest of mankind. But God, being rich in mercy, because of the great love with which he loved us, even when we were dead in our trespasses, made us alive together with Christ—by grace you have been saved— and raised us up with him and seated us with him in the heavenly places in Christ Jesus, so that in the coming ages he might show the immeasurable riches of his grace in kindness toward us in Christ

Jesus. For by grace you have been saved through faith. And this is not your own doing; it is the gift of God, not a result of works, so that no one may boast. For we are his workmanship, created in Christ Jesus for good works, which God prepared beforehand, that we should walk in them. (Eph. 2:1–10)

This chapter immediately follows Paul's introduction of the concept of predestination in chapter 1, and he now labors the point that God quickens people while they are still spiritually dead in sin and trespasses. This is why the two metaphors earlier described are not biblically accurate. The drowning man—no matter how desperate his situation as he's about to sink and with only his fingers are above the waves—is still alive. That is not the metaphor of Scripture.

The metaphor of Scripture is that the man has *already* drowned. He is at the bottom of the ocean. The New Testament teaches that God the Holy Spirit is like a rescuer who dives to the bottom of the sea, pulls the dead man out, and breathes life into him. Likewise, the dying man in the hospital who has to open his mouth to receive the medicine is not really desperately and critically ill. He is already dead. Taking life-saving medicine to the coroner's office or the morgue and offering it to a corpse is an exercise in futility. A corpse cannot open its mouth to receive healing medicine. The person has died, and only God can make him alive.

The problem with the prescient view of election is that it has God looking down through the corridors of time at people who are spiritually dead. If God looked at people who were dead in sin, even if He looked for a long time, how many would He find responding positively to the gospel? He would have no one to elect, no one to predestine, because He would see all of them perishing in their unbelief. Jesus said to Nicodemus, "Truly, truly, I say to you, unless one is born again he cannot see the kingdom of God" (John 3:3).

Later in the gospel of John, we read:

But Jesus, knowing in himself that his disciples were grumbling about this, said to them, "Do you take offense at this? Then what if you were to see the Son of Man ascending to where he was before? It is the Spirit who gives life; the flesh is no help at all. The words that I have spoken to you are spirit and life. But there are some of you who do not believe." (For Jesus knew from the beginning who those were who did not believe, and who it was who would betray him.) And he said, "This is why I told you that no one can come to me unless it is granted him by the Father." (John 6:61–63, 65)

Jesus says the flesh is no help at all; it profits nothing. It does not contribute even 1 percent; it contributes 0 percent. One hundred percent of our salvation is from God.

If the Bible never mentioned the words *predestination* or *election*, we would still be driven to conclude that concept simply from the abundant references we find in the Scriptures about the state of our moral condition apart from saving grace and regeneration. The biggest hurdle we have to get over—before we are ready to assign the fullness of grace to our salvation—is the hurdle of thinking that we really do have an island of righteousness left in our souls that is unaffected by the fall and unpolluted by sin. It is the false belief that we're not really dead in sin and trespasses, but that we're only sick in sin and trespasses, still possessing the ability to revive ourselves once we hear the gospel. If we want to overcome these hurdles, we must truly understand the absolute sinfulness of sin and the absolute graciousness of grace.

Chapter Eight

The Other Side
of the Coin

One of the controversies that attends any discussion of the doctrine of predestination involves the question of so-called double predestination. We've already considered the wonder of God's mercy and grace as He unilaterally intrudes into the lives of sinners, snatching them from the fire and bringing them safely home to heaven. But we also must ask, What about those who do not receive that gift? What about those who do not receive regeneration? In other words: What about those who are not elect?

Various views have been offered in an attempt to answer this question. Some argue for single predestination. This means that from all eternity, God has chosen to intervene in the lives of some people to bring them to faith through a special act of grace, but at the same time, He does not choose or decree anything at all concerning the salvation or damnation of those who are not elect. Some say that those who are not elect still have the opportunity to be saved if they want to be saved, but in any case, only the elect will certainly be saved.

Part of the problem is that some people have a distorted understanding of predestination and election. They think of it as if God drags people kicking and screaming against their wills into the kingdom of God, and at the same time He prevents other people from coming to the kingdom who do want to be there. Let's address the first part of this idea, that God drags unwilling people into the kingdom.

The Augustinian doctrine of election unto salvation says this: no one wants Christ. No one wants to come into the kingdom of God. The heart is desperately wicked, and it desires only evil continuously. "No one seeks for God," the Apostle Paul quoted (Rom. 3:11). If left to our own desires and inclinations, none of us would ever incline ourselves to come to Christ. So, in our natural state, none of us wants to enter the kingdom of God.

Does that mean that God drags us kicking and screaming into the kingdom? No, and the reason is that we have been regenerated. For us to be saved, God must first regenerate us. Regeneration is the raising to new spiritual life; it is a change in the disposition of hearts. Before regeneration, we don't want anything to do with Christ; afterward, we love Him. God the Holy Spirit creates that love in our hearts. The Spirit makes us willing, so that we then choose Christ, and we choose Christ because we want Christ. Therefore, no one is dragged kicking and screaming into the kingdom; everyone who enters the kingdom desires to be there.

The second aspect of the distorted idea of predestination is that God keeps people out of the kingdom who desperately want to be there. But, as we have seen, *no one* in his natural state wants to be there. We are fugitives from God. There is no one who wants God whom God excludes from the kingdom. In fact, if someone wants to come to the biblical Christ, that is the surest evidence that he is numbered among the elect, not the reprobate.

The question of double predestination concerns not

only the positive side of the coin (election), but also the negative side, which we call reprobation. Reprobation is the opposite of election. Someone who is reprobate has not been chosen and does not receive the benefit of saving grace. Unless we are universalists (meaning we believe that everyone is predestined to salvation), we have no option but to affirm some kind of reprobation. If some are chosen but not all receive that gift, then obviously some are not elect. Unless everyone is elect, we have two categories—the elect and the nonelect. And because two categories exist, there must be some kind of double predestination. What is the correct understanding of the doctrine of double predestination?

One view of double predestination is called the symmetrical view. This view teaches that God operates in the lives of the reprobate in the same way that He operates in the lives of the elect in that He is *active* when addressing the reprobate. With respect to the elect, God, through His power and the agency of His Holy Spirit, is active in unilaterally creating faith in their hearts. With respect to the reprobate, God is active in creating fresh evil in their souls and in forcing them directly and immediately to reject the gospel because He doesn't want them in His kingdom.

According to this view, God forces people to sin by His direct intervention. This is called a *positive-positive* view of predestination, because God acts positively and actively toward both the elect and the reprobate.

By contrast, the Augustinian view of double predestination is asymmetrical. It is called a *positive-negative* view of predestination. This view holds that God does a positive work in the lives of the elect whereby He intervenes to rescue them from spiritual death by making them alive and creating faith in their souls. With respect to the reprobate, God does not do a positive work by creating fresh evil in their hearts and forcing them to reject Christ. Rather, He does a negative work by merely passing over them. He performs what is often described in the New Testament as a type of divine punishment, wherein He gives sinners over to their sinful dispositions and abandons them to their sin. He ceases to restrain them from their own evil ways. God doesn't have to create unbelief or wickedness in the hearts of the reprobate; it's already there.

When God elects unto salvation, He elects out of a mass of humanity that together is fallen, dead in sin and trespasses. By His gracious act of intervention, He steps in to accomplish a saving work in the hearts of some that

He does not accomplish for the others. He doesn't prevent the others from coming to Christ—He doesn't *have* to prevent them from coming to Christ. They prevent themselves because they don't want to come to Christ. They are already alienated from God, dead in their sins and trespasses. God does not force them to say no to Christ and the gospel; they reject Christ out of their own inclinations, their own hearts, their own wills. They do not come to Christ because they do not want to come to Christ.

This positive-negative view brings us back to the example of Jacob and Esau as an illustration of the elect and nonelect. Jacob received a blessing of God's grace that Esau did not, and Jacob received that blessing not because of anything that he did or willed to do. The decision was made by God before Jacob and Esau were born or had done anything good or bad. In his response to this example, the Apostle Paul reminds his readers of God's sovereign authority and right to dispose His grace however He sees fit: "I will have mercy on whom I have mercy" (Rom. 9:15). Double predestination is simply this: the elect receive mercy and the reprobate receive justice, but no one receives injustice.

One of the difficulties we have in wrestling with the doctrine of election is that we are not privy to the inner thoughts of God's mind, except insofar as He is pleased to reveal them in sacred Scripture. We don't know why He doesn't choose to elect all people; we just know that He doesn't. We don't know why He has grace and mercy on some to a special degree that He doesn't lavish on everyone. But as Calvin remarked, "Where God closes His holy mouth, I will desist from inquiry."

The prescient view is ultimately a very pessimistic perspective to hold. In this view, God leaves everyone to themselves. He merely issues an outward call without granting a direct, gracious change to people's hearts. The Augustinian view more highly exalts the mercy and grace of God as He sovereignly changes sinners' hearts, enabling them to see the beauty and truth of Christ and His gospel and compelling them to respond in faith and obedience.

Chapter Nine

Beautiful Feet

Most discussions about predestination and election eventually turn into a debate on the topic of evangelism. Two primary objections commonly arise. The first is that if predestination is true, then there is no need to evangelize. After all, those who are elect will be saved one way or the other, and those who are not elect cannot be saved, regardless of how much effort we exert in evangelism. The other is the accusation that those who believe in predestination are characteristically unconcerned about evangelism and inhibit the church's mission in that regard.

This second objection is easy to answer: it's simply not true. History bears witness that it is not true. Looking at early American history shows that evangelistic activity in the Colonies was unprecedented. During the First Great Awakening—in which God richly poured out His Holy Spirit, particularly on New England—three chief preachers were used of God as instruments of evangelism. One of them, John Wesley, did not embrace the Augustinian view of election unto salvation, but the other two, George Whitefield and Jonathan Edwards, wholeheartedly embraced it.

During the Reformation in the sixteenth century, the gospel went out around the world. Martin Luther, John Calvin, John Knox, and Huldrych Zwingli were totally committed to the Augustinian view of predestination. William Carey held to the Augustinian view and carried the gospel to India. Charles Spurgeon in nineteenth-century England had the same commitment to the Augustinian view. And closer to our time, D. James Kennedy, a strong advocate of the Augustinian view, designed Evangelism Explosion, which has been used worldwide and has shown countless people their need for Christ. This record shows that embracing the biblical doctrine of election does not in any way inhibit evangelism.

However, the first objection remains: If predestination is true, why evangelize? One answer is simple: God, in His Word, has commanded us to evangelize. How can a person believe in election but not believe in the sovereignty of God? More specifically, how can a person believe in the sovereignty of God and despise the mandate of a sovereign God? God is sovereign not only in His grace but also in His commands, and He commands us to preach the gospel to every living creature.

This command is not based on the assumption that we are desperately needed by God, and that without our contribution, His salvific purposes couldn't come to pass. Rather, the efforts we employ in the preaching of the gospel and the work of evangelism can only be fruitful by His sovereign grace. The Apostle Paul made that clear when he said, "I planted, Apollos watered, but God gave the growth" (1 Cor. 3:6). Of course, God could have brought the growth without Paul's planting or Apollos' watering, but with respect to predestination, God not only foreordains ends, He also foreordains the means to that end.

What is the chief means that God uses to bring about salvation for His elect? According to Scripture, God has chosen the foolishness of preaching to save the world.

Paul himself, the great advocate of predestination, declared, "For I am not ashamed of the gospel, for it is the power of God for salvation to everyone who believes, to the Jew first and also to the Greek" (Rom. 1:16). He later says that "faith comes from hearing, and hearing through the word of Christ" (10:17). This Word has been entrusted to His church, and it is the mission of the church to proclaim and preach, to plant and water, always knowing that the increase belongs to the Lord.

We have established that it is the Christian's duty to be engaged in evangelism. However, we cannot simply stop at this principle of duty. Evangelism is not just a duty but a privilege. It is an incredible thing that God would choose to use us to be instruments in His hand to proclaim the gospel and to bring the Word that elicits faith through the work of the Holy Spirit. The very planting and watering we do is used as a part of His plan to redeem His people. He could do it without us. He certainly doesn't need us, yet He gives us the unspeakable privilege of participating in this work.

Romans 10:10–15 declares:

For with the heart one believes and is justified, and with the mouth one confesses and is saved. For the Scripture says, "Everyone who believes in him will not be put to shame." For there is no distinction between Jew and Greek; for the same Lord is Lord of all, bestowing his riches on all who call on him. For "everyone who calls on the name of the Lord will be saved." How then will they call on him in whom they have not believed? And how are they to believe in him of whom they have never heard? And how are they to hear without someone preaching? And how are they to preach unless they are sent? As it is written, "How beautiful are the feet of those who preach the good news!"

This is a classic text for missions. The word *mission* comes from the Latin *missio*, which means "to send." A missionary is sent by the church for a purpose: to proclaim the gospel so that people may hear and come to faith. God has not put in our hands the power to change a heart of stone into a heart of flesh, but we do have the ability to open our mouths, confess our faith, and proclaim the Scriptures, which God uses to bring faith to His people.

People cannot have faith if they don't have anything to believe in. They cannot believe in something they've never heard, and they can't hear unless someone tells them. There is no hearing without a preacher being sent. Paul then quotes a very important passage from the Old Testament: "As it is written, 'How beautiful are the feet of those who preach the good news!'" (Rom. 10:15). This Old Testament text, abbreviated in Romans, occurs in the book of Isaiah: "How beautiful upon the mountains are the feet of him who brings good news, who publishes peace, who brings good news of happiness, who publishes salvation, who says to Zion, 'Your God reigns'" (Isa. 52:7).

In the ancient world, there were no cell phones and no internet. The only way to spread news was to have someone carry it. So, for instance, when a great battle was going on, the only way for the people at home to know how the battle was going was to have someone run back to the city and deliver the news. This is why we have races today called marathons. According to tradition, after the Battle of Marathon in 490 BC, a runner traveled 26.2 miles back to Athens to tell of the Athenians' victory over the Persians.

Cities would post lookouts on their walls who would scan the distance for the approach of a runner. Before they could see the look on the runner's face, they could tell by his footfalls in the distance whether he was bringing good news or bad news. The bearer of bad news would not have his feet flying in great joy. When the Battle of Marathon runner approached the city gates, his feet kicking up the dust, they could tell by his feet alone that the news was good news.

The prophet Isaiah borrows that imagery, for the custom of bearing news by messenger was the custom in the Old Testament as well. Isaiah says, "How beautiful upon the mountains are the feet of him who brings good news, who publishes peace."

I became a Christian in 1957 when an upperclassman college football player explained the identity of Christ to me. That night changed my life forever. I will be eternally grateful for his ministry in my life. To me, his feet are beautiful. He took the time to tell me about Christ. Of course, God could have used someone else to bring me to saving faith. He didn't need to use the testimony of my friend, and I know that ultimately I owe my salvation not to my friend but to God. Salvation is of the Lord. Yet on this earthly, horizontal plane, in this arena of human activity, I have profound affection and gratitude for those God uses as His instruments of evangelism. What a privilege to be used by God to bring another person to Christ.

If you're a Christian, think about the people in your life whom God used to bring you to Christ or help you grow in your faith. Pray for them. Reach out and thank them. Many times, we aren't even aware that God has used us in others' lives unless they tell us so. Thank the people who have been used by God to open your eyes to the riches of Christ, and let us likewise go out in joy and obedience to publish the good news of the gospel of God's salvation.

About the Author

Dr. R.C. Sproul was founder of Ligonier Ministries, founding pastor of Saint Andrew's Chapel in Sanford, Fla., first president of Reformation Bible College, and executive editor of *Tabletalk* magazine. His radio program, *Renewing Your Mind,* is still broadcast daily on hundreds of radio stations around the world and can also be heard online. He was author of more than one hundred books, including *The Holiness of God, Chosen by God,* and *Everyone's a Theologian.* He was recognized throughout the world for his articulate defense of the inerrancy of Scripture and the need for God's people to stand with conviction upon His Word.

Get 3 free months
of *Tabletalk*

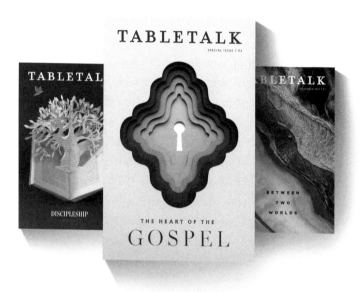

In 1977, R.C. Sproul started *Tabletalk* magazine.
Today it has become the most widely read subscriber-based monthly
devotional magazine in the world. **Try it free for 3 months.**

TryTabletalk.com/CQ | 800.435.4343